Love TO LET GO

LOVING OUR KIDS INTO ADULTHOOD

Jack Stoltzfus Ph.D.

Love to Let Go: Loving Our Kids into Adulthood

This is the second in a series of books on parental practices that help support the young adult's task of independence.

Can You Speak Millennial "ese"? How to Understand and Communicate with Your Young Adult
Love to Let Go: Loving Our Kids into Adulthood
Apology: The Gift We Give Our Young Adults
Forgiveness: The Gift We Share with Our Young Adults and Ourselves
Supportive Integrity: Parenting Our Young Adults with Love and Backbone
Growing Apart: Letting Go of Our Young Adults

ISBN 978-0-9994563-1-6

Dr. Jack Stoltzfus
www.parentslettinggo.com

Contents

Preface

Love to Let Go is the second in a series of books describing the six practices parents need to undertake to effectively launch their young adult. It is about **unconditional love**. The first practice described in *Can You Speak "Millennial "ese"* is about **understanding** your young adult. Both practices are foundational to being the best parent you can be in helping your young adult successfully move toward behavioral and emotional independence. Subsequent books will address the other four practices essential to launching one's young adult: apology, forgiveness, supportive integrity, and letting go.

The books and the website (www.parentslettinggo.com) arose out of a need I discovered in my work as a psychologist with a growing number of clients. These were parents of adult children struggling with efforts to balance support and letting go. This segment of parents is a forgotten group who have experienced both more closeness with their millennial children but also more difficulty assisting them in leaving the nest. I'm also in this forgotten group as I have raised three married young adult children.

Although I lamented the absence of help for this group of parents and wondered why there wasn't more, I eventually decided to step up and begin to create some resources. Initially this was in the form of a workshop delivered locally in Shoreview, Minnesota. That grew to the development of a website, books, and other materials. This book is one resource that outlines the case for loving emancipation and offers very practical actions parents can take to carry this out. I argue that without the continued loving connection with parents, these young adults will flounder in their search for healthy independence.

When you start reading this book, you will see unconditional love is only one practice that needs to be undertaken by parents in becoming more effective with the launch process. Please keep this in mind. Unconditional love is not the whole story. But it is a critical, essential practice that secures the relationship so the young adult feels safe and supported in moving into emotional and behavioral independence.

About the Author

Dr. Jack Stoltzfus is a licensed psychologist practicing in Shoreview, Minnesota. He received his PhD in counseling psychology from the University of Wisconsin-Madison. The focus of his PhD dissertation was on defining and measuring healthy adolescent separation from parents. His private practice is focused on parents and young adults. Dr. Stoltzfus has worked with parents and their young adult children within the context of a chemical dependency day treatment program, inpatient mental health facilities, a child guidance clinic, a youth service agency, and a private practice for more than thirty years. He has three grown and married young adult children who represent the millennial and early Gen X generations.

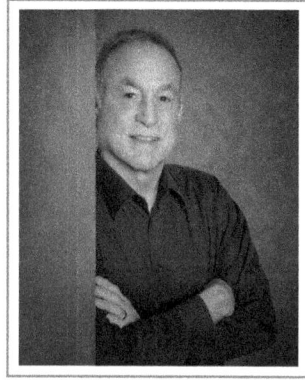

CHAPTER 1

Do You Love Me?

"Would you cry if I died?" the angry teenager asked in a hushed and hesitant voice as he sat across from his burly father in the therapist's office.

The father looked deeply into his son's eyes and said, "There are not enough buckets in the world to hold the tears I would shed if something happened to you."

My colleague Diane Dovenberg told me this story when we were clinicians at Wilder Child Guidance Clinic. It speaks to the questions that children of all ages have and want to ask: Do I matter to you? Do you love me in spite of my actions or ways I may have disappointed or continue to disappoint you? Do you love me unconditionally?

CHAPTER 2

What Is Unconditional Love?

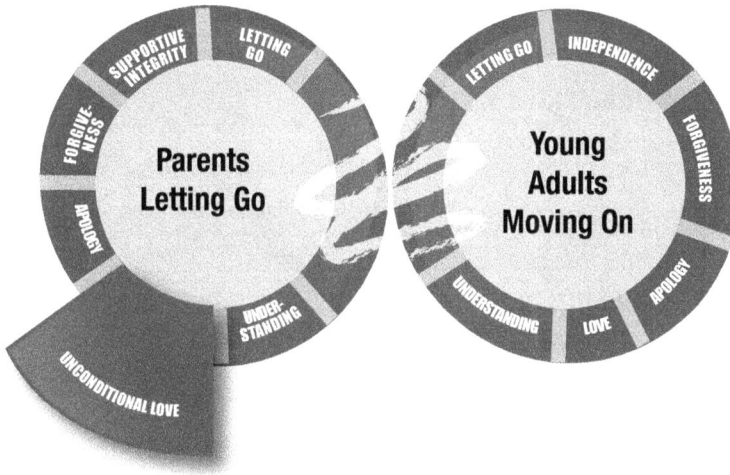

The second foundational practice, beyond understanding your young adult, is that of securing your relationship with them by demonstrating the love you hold for them. This practice assures your young adult that they have a base of support and love upon which they can venture forth. The diagram highlights this practice. As this practice is emphasized, there is both an increased potential for greater success in the launch process as well as continued dialogue. The white squiggly lines refer to a continued level of communication and connection between the parent and the young adult while allowing both to experience full autonomy.

What words, phases, or descriptors come to mind when you think of unconditional love?

_____

_____

_____

_____

Unconditional love of a parent for the child is foundational to support the development process, not just during infancy but throughout life, and is critical to facilitating the separation process of young adulthood. Beyond the value to the launching process, unconditional love of a parent for a child can be life sustaining and life saving. If a young adult knows they can hold onto a belief that they are loved, even if they feel that their life may be falling apart, that love can enable them to keep going. And in the darkest moments of despair, knowing they have parents or a parent whose love for them is unwavering can convince them that their life is worth living.

Unconditional love is an unchanging affection that knows no bounds, conditions, or limitations. The model of unconditional love that comes to mind for many is that oxytocin-charged bonding between a new mother and her infant. Although I can't speak to this experience from the mother's standpoint, I can say that as a father I became deeply attached to my children, not instantly, but over their first months as we were able to connect and communicate.

After my wife and I had a child, I discovered qualities of deep love, attachment, responsibility, and protectiveness that I had never felt before. It seemed to come out of nowhere and was surprising to me. And it continued with each subsequent child. What it speaks to is the belief that we are hardwired to love our children. It is as important for us as parents to express this love as it is for our children to experience it. When we don't express this love, we, at best, live a diminished life and damage not only ourselves but our children and our relationship with them. And this need to express and to receive unconditional love doesn't stop with adulthood.

"A deep sense of love and belonging is an irreducible need of all women, men and children. We are biologically and spiritually wired to love, be loved and to belong. When these needs are not met, we don't function as we were meant to. We break. We fall apart. We numb. We ache. We hurt others. We get sick."[1]

—*The Gifts of Imperfection*, Brene Brown

The Characteristics of Unconditional Love

- Love between a parent and a child is hardwired into us at birth. Withdrawing our love from our young adults damages our relationship and wounds both the parent and the child. When children don't experience this love, it undermines their faith in us and in life.

- Love for a child endures no matter what. It doesn't stop even if a parent has lost a child.

In the late 1990s, as I managed a health promotion program at 3M Company, I discovered a group of parents in 3M who were living with the constant grief of losing a child. So I helped to organize the first Compassionate Friends Group in a corporate setting. Compassionate Friends is a national organization that supports parents who have experienced the death of a child. In our small group meeting, the level of grief of these parents, some of whom had lost a child more than ten years previously, was overwhelming. We passed the tissue box around as these parents shared their grief and their enduring love for their child. Although I have not lost a child, I took my turn with the tissue box. As the saying goes: "Lose your parents, lose your past; lose your spouse, lose your present; lose your child, lose your future."

- Unconditional love exists "in spite of" not "because of." It may not be easy or make sense to love someone who is abusive, but you can see past your child's behavior to the goodness that lies within.

- It comes from the lover and not the loved. It is not dependent on the person loved in some type of quid pro quo way. This may be the most challenging expectation for some parents. We are challenged to rise above feelings of blame and rejection and continue to reach out in love. Not just for the sake of our children but for our sake.

- It is action and not just feelings or words. Words are necessary but not sufficient. They have to be backed up by actions that demonstrate this love. Love has to be a verb.

Too often we use the phase "I love you but . . ." The "but" basically negates the first part of the sentence. The receiver of the message hears the exception and that the "love you" doesn't really apply unless we comply with what follows the "but."

- Unconditional love puts the other first. It's not done to feed the parent's need to feel loved or make the parent feel they are a good parent. It is done for the benefit of the child. A good question to ask when connecting with an adult child is: "Am I doing this because it will primarily help my young adult or help me?" How will you know your motive? Pay attention to your reaction if your young adult doesn't follow your advice, reciprocate, demonstrate appreciation, and so forth. If you feel hurt, angry, resentful, or frustrated, it could be more about your own needs.

- It is expressed in vulnerable, sincere ways and there is a risk of rejection. Even for some parents there is risk in expressing one's feelings of love. Will the young adult reject it, question it, or use it to extract some concessions? "If you love me then . . ." Unconditional love involves risk and the possibility of suffering.

We suffer in love when we see our young adult suffering and recognize we can't make it better. Don't we always want to "make it better"?

- Unconditional love defies or overrides our cultural, dualistic tendencies to sort actions into right and wrong, deserved or not deserved. Unconditional love overrides all qualifications and judgments.

CHAPTER 4

Unconditional Love Is Not Unconditional Approval

Some parents may confuse unconditional love with unconditional approval, and these are two different concepts. You can be unconditionally loving of the person but not their behavior or attitude. Here us what unconditional love is not.

1. It is not accepting or approving of the behavior of your young adult, particularly if it is counter to your core values.

   I had an affluent family I saw in my private practice who had denied their sixteen-year-old son some privilege, such as the use of the car. Out of anger this son took a morning star ninja weapon, chained ball of sharp steel protrusions, and raked the house and furniture with it. Unconditional love calls the police.

2. It is not giving into their requests or demands if you do not agree with them. "Enabling" is not unconditional love. The word *enabling* has come to be used in the field of chemical dependency and codependence to describe actions by a caring person to support irresponsible behavior of another or spare that person from the consequence of their behavior.

3. When our young adults were toddlers we didn't support them playing in the street. As adults, why would we support, condone, or look the other way with their drug habit or other destructive actions. Love in action may require us to say "no" but not give up loving them as a person. A later practice book, *No Is Not a Four-Letter Word*, will address the importance of integrity and the fact that "no" may be the most empowering and loving thing you can say.

4. Unconditional love is not earned.

5. It is not the same as romantic love. Romantic love is dependent on the response of another and often charged with hormones and dopamine surges.

6. It doesn't depend on the reaction or anticipated reaction of the other.

7. Unconditional love is not blind. It doesn't ignore the behavior of the child that is self-destructive or inappropriate. It sees through the flaws and shortcomings to the deeper worth of the person.

8. It is necessary but not sufficient to influence the young adult's behavior and should not be given with this end in mind. It doesn't teach children about the conditionality of the world. Frank Farrelly, a therapist in Madison, Wisconsin, said that in traditional families, mothers, for the most part, taught kids unconditional love. No matter what they do they are loved. Fathers in these traditional families taught kids about conditional love.[2] Essentially there is no free lunch once you leave home. Both mothers and fathers need to demonstrate unconditional love and both need to speak to the reality of the world that is conditional. Splitting up these lessons for children and young adults between the parents undermines the development of children and the healthy relationship with each parent. Alfie Kohn in *Unconditional Parenting* makes the best case I have read for the unconditional loving side of parenting.[3] A later book in this series, *Supportive Integrity:*

Parenting Our Young Adults with Love and Backbone, addresses the subject of setting limits, taking a stand, and integrity—the conditional side of parenting.

9. It is not dependent on our feelings at any given point in time; it's a commitment and an action.

10. It does not control, guilt, threaten, bind, or suffocate the young adult. Statements that start with "Because I love you . . ." followed by an expectation or request are not expressions of unconditional love; they undermine it.

CHAPTER 5

The Importance of Unconditional Love

- **It creates a sense of safety and security;** it is a holding, container, or placeholder in our lives. We feel we belong in this world. We are wired for relationships, as Daniel Siegel says in his book *Mindsight*,[4] and we feel secure when we are loved, no matter what the age.

- **It is the most significant antidote to "shame."** Shame is the sense that one is fundamentally flawed. When someone feels shame they don't believe they should be alive. They believe they are fundamentally defective. When parents express unconditional love for the young person regardless of their actions, it says they belong and have immense value to the parent.

    I had a friend who told me that he found out as a teenager his mother had tried to abort him during her pregnancy. She tried using a saline solution and jumping off a chair. What a message to have to live with—your mother tried to stamp out your life before you were born. Although the mother did try to raise this young man with love, the fact that he was not wanted at birth continued to have damaging repercussions in his life and relationships.

- The young adult who experiences unconditional love believes that he has a **guarantor—someone who guarantees his existence**. This is a concept that one of my mentors, Bill Smith, shared with me. It is about standing with and behind them in their life journey, but letting them live "their" dream not ours. Parents often will say: "We will be here for you." The importance is to support young adults emotionally and help them find solutions to challenges they face—not just to write a check or provide some other material need.

- **It affirms not just their doing but also their being.** We love them no matter what. Sue Kliebold, mother of Dylan Kliebold who shot and killed thirteen people at Columbine High School, says in her book *A Mother's Reckoning* "that she would never stop loving Dylan. I didn't have any other way of responding to him but to love him. That's what parents do."[5] Our young adults need to know that our love for them as our children is enduring and nothing they do can take this away.

- **Unconditional love frees children** to risk, explore, try, and fail knowing that these actions, mistakes, and failures will not define their worth.

- **It is the most important gift and modeling** we can give our children.

- **It begins with the attachment experience in childhood.**

> *"If pure, eternal, unconditional love is the foundation on which you stand, even if all else falls away, you are still valuable because you are loved."*
>
> —Amy Lichtenhan

CHAPTER 6

Secure Childhood Attachment as Unconditional Love

The need to connect with another human being is hardwired and begins with the experience of attachment to a primary caregiver, usually the mother. This bonding affects brain development, self-esteem, resilience, and the quality of relationships later in life. John Bowlby, an English psychiatrist, and Mary Ainsworth, an American psychologist, brought attention to the importance of this early bonding experience to later adjustment in life. Their work and subsequent scientific studies have identified the benefits of healthy attachment and the repercussions of failed attachment experiences.

It is clear that adults who have experienced secure attachment feel safe and secure. They are capable of empathy and develop intimate, meaningful relationships. They effectively manage their emotions and stress and are willing to explore and venture forth in life. Failure by the caregiver to exhibit healthy, secure attachment engendering behavior can lead to difficulties for the young adult later in life. These may include avoidance of closeness and emotional contact, anxious behavior, over-reaction, distrust, erratic mood swings, and tendencies toward feelings of rejection, criticism, and blame of others and self. The young adult characteristics of a failure to form a healthy connection or bond with the parents in the launching years may include behaviors such as anger, reactivity, blaming, protesting, depression, withdrawal, acting out, drugs, illegal activities, rejection of parents, fear, and dependency.

> *"Maybe I didn't do the best job of ensuring that my child was attached. Is my child doomed for life and is our relationship irreparable?" a mother asks.*

Don't Blame Mother

Every since the days of Freud, there has been a tendency to blame "mother" for all of the shortcomings and problems of the offspring. Clearly this is not true, so please don't get carried away at this point if you believe that you may have not had the best early attachment experience with your young adult child. Most parents already have a lot of guilt related to their parenting, so don't think you are responsible for all of the behavior of your young adult child—good or bad. Even worse is to believe you are responsible for fixing your adult child's behavior.

Many other factors in the development of the child including temperament, later childhood experiences, and peer influences come into play in the choices and actions of young adults. The simple fact that young adults can choose to do what they want, and not chose wisely, can contribute to challenges at this stage of life. Parents often do a good job of training their children to think for themselves only to find that when they do—and it doesn't meet parental expectations—they're upset. At some point, parents have to let go of the notion that they are responsible for and/or can control their young adult's behavior. If society believes the young adult is responsible to sign contracts, serve the military, vote, and so forth, shouldn't parents believe they are responsible for their *actions* as well? This part of letting go will be addressed in the last practice book, *Growing Apart*.

You Can't Change the Past

Although a parent can't go back and change the past, there are actions that you can take now to secure the relationship with your young adult and provide the foundation they need to successfully attain emotional and behavioral independence. Furthermore, as children move into young adulthood, they need to take greater responsibility for their lives regardless of their family history. Early attachment difficulties and childhood experiences may explain some later in life difficulties but don't excuse them.

It's not helpful to excuse young adult behavior because you feel guilty about something that happened in your parenting of the child. Or to be held ransom by your young adult for something you did or didn't do in their growing up years. The best you can do is to say you are sorry, ask for their forgiveness, and move on. The next book in this series, *Apology: The Gift We Give Our Young Adults*, describes the practices of apology and forgiveness that are essential to putting the past behind. These practices may be necessary for you to be able to effectively communicate your love for your young adult. Like expressing love, however, words will not be enough. If there are some behaviors that you regret but they continue, saying you are sorry will be seen as insincere. Focus on what you can do to enhance the bond between you and your young adult so that they experience the safety and security to venture into the world successfully.

CHAPTER 7

Secure Attachment and the Young Adult—My Story

Attachment and emotional bonds are important throughout the family life cycle. Having a positive attachment to parents creates the safety and security needed to move toward independence. Parents with children at the adolescent and young adult stage need not withdraw love and affection for the young adult but pair it with letting go of control. The closeness of the parents to the young adult aids the separation process not unlike the infant attachment experience. In fact, this adolescent/young adult time is often described as the second individuation (separation) process. The infant and toddler experience the trust and safety of the parent that enables the child to explore new areas of the room and extend the orbit from the parent. Likewise the adolescent/young adult who experiences the love and affection (attachment to the parents) can move out to new experiences such as work, education, intimate relationships, travel, and so forth. When both parents and the young adult move closer in love, both experience more freedom.

> *The words differentiation and individuation describe the attainment of a healthy emotional and behavioral independence from parents. These words are common in adolescent/young adult developmental literature.*

Let me tell you about my own experience in moving closer to my father as a way to experience more freedom. Think about your young adult or reflect on your young adult experience with your father or mother. There are two reasons for sharing this story. First, I want you to learn something of what one young adult experience—mine—was like so you may be able to empathize with your young adult. Second, the process I used to address the gap between my father and me is the same process I am suggesting for parents. Either party can move to close a gap and in doing so free both.

At the age of twenty-five, I began to face the anger and resentment I felt for my father. Although I was independent, physically and financially, living more than twelve hundred miles from my parents, I was not emotionally independent. If you are living with a variety of painful emotions toward a parent, you are not differentiated and not healthy. Such unresolved emotions creep into other relationships, in my case particularly relationships with authority figures—professors and managers. Fortunately for me I was enrolled in a masters pro-gram in counseling psychology and began to realize that such unre-solved feelings toward my father would be detrimental to my work as a psychologist, not to mention my relationships in general.

Although my father was a good person and never abusive to me, the relationship had become estranged over the years as each of us pulled further away from the other. My infrequent visits home were typically characterized by some degree of conflict or reaction on my part to something my father would say, particularly if it were critical in tone. On one visit my mother asked why I didn't talk to my dad more. My angry response was: "Why doesn't he talk to me?" After making this comment and storming out of the kitchen, I started walking down the alley and found myself sobbing. The anger was sit-ting on top of a deep hurt and sense of rejection, and the longing for an accepting and close relationship with my father that didn't exist.

There was a significant lack of bonding between my father and me that was related to this sense of rejection and a question of his love for me. On one visit home in my early twenties, I proudly arrived sprouting a sorry excuse for a beard. When my father saw this he refused to speak to me. He viewed growing a beard as reflective of rebellion. I proposed that our ancestors had beards, but this was not well received. I had to ask my mother to ask my dad to pass the butter. Upon later reflection on my father's behavior, I began to realize this is something he no doubt experienced or observed in his growing up. His father, my great grandfather, and other relatives were all of Amish descent. In the Amish tradition if a child or member of the community violated the norms they were shunned. Shunning involved a withdrawing of fellowship from a member who had violated certain norms, essentially acting as if they didn't exist.

This rejection by my father on such a small matter and the fact that he had never told me he loved me, left me insecure about his love and our relationship. I thought if I ever did anything egregious and ended up in prison, he would never come to see me and essentially disown me. Although, like most young adults, I viewed the gap between my father and me as primarily his fault, I decided for my own well being to take the initiative to address this.

The process for me was a two-step process, and I would argue it could be the same for a parent who would take the initiative.

First I sat down and wrote a letter to my father detailing my many grievances with him over the twenty-five years. As I did this initially, I indicted my father for not reaching out to me emotionally, criticizing and rejecting me on more than one occasion. At some point I connected to the underlying hurt and sense of rejection and the tears came to my eyes. This took several hours but clearly identified the sense of lost connection with my father and my unexpressed love to him. I ended the letter with a statement of my forgiveness for him not reaching out to me more. There was a level of empathy preceding this forgiveness that arose out of understanding the limitations my father experienced with his father. Empathy is the route to forgiveness. As to that letter, it didn't serve a purpose to send it to him; it was for my benefit. It was something I needed to do for myself. I needed to let go of the hurt and resentment and did this through expressing those feelings and forgiveness. The act of forgiveness also represented an acknowledgment that I was part of the distance problem, particularly in my young adult years. This cathartic exercise of letting go of my resentment and embracing forgiveness served to free me from the hold these thoughts and feelings had on me and as such the letter was best sent to the shredder.

As Rabbi Kushner, the author of *When Bad Things Happen to Good People,* said in a radio broadcast: Forgiveness is the favor you give yourself.6 It was a gift to me to release emotions and thoughts that had kept me negatively fused to my father and caused the reactivity that arose out of our interactions. More often then not the feelings that need to be released by parents are guilt, regret, mistakes made, or failures to be the parent they wanted to be. The next practice book, *Apology: The Gift We Give Our Young Adults*, will explore how parents let go of these and other negative feelings that bind them in unhealthy ways to their young adults.

The second step was to express my love for my father now that I had cleared out all the underlying anger, resentment, and hurt. This became a more difficult task than I thought for a couple of reasons. One was that my father had never told me he loved me, which left me in some state of doubt and insecurity. And I had never told him I loved him. Part of me wanted to protest and say that he should be the one to communicate this to me first. For me to do this was to break a rule in the family in which such direct expressions of love and affection were absent. But I decided not to wait.

On one of my visits, I drove my father to the airport for a business trip and prepared my speech to him while driving. I remember my hands being somewhat sweaty on the steering wheel as I rehearsed what I was planning to say. I decided not to say this to him in the car. It felt too confining and uncomfortable since neither of us could escape the scene if it didn't go well. As I helped him pull his luggage out of the trunk of the car, I said to him, "Dad, I just want you to know I love you." There was an immediate release of emotion and awareness that I no longer felt this burden of defensiveness or reactivity.

You may wonder what my father said back to me. I'd like to say he reached out, embraced me, and said he loved me and always has and will. Unfortunately, he gave the classic two-headed parent reply of his generation: "Your mother and I love you too." Not exactly what I wanted, but I had determined that no matter what his response was, I needed to communicate my love to him. I had no expectation related to his response. What he said or didn't say didn't diminish the sense of freedom I experienced in expressing my feelings toward him. When I flew back to my home in Minneapolis, I sat down and wrote him a letter describing my experience of working through my feelings for him including referencing my private letter, which I had destroyed, and my uncomfortable but sincere effort to express my love for him. Shortly thereafter he acknowledged the letter and expressed his love for me directly on a phone conversation.

The story has a bittersweet ending. Two years later I got a tearful call from my mother saying that my dad had died of a sudden heart attack at the age of sixty-six. He had no cardiac history and was not a smoker, drinker, or overweight. We were all in a state of shock and disbelief. In attending the funeral, I found myself sobbing not for the loss of my father, but for the loss of the years of closeness we never had.

Sometimes we grieve what we never had more than what we had. The bittersweet part is that, thankfully, we had this time of reconciliation and closeness in my father's final years. But we had both lost out on the closeness we wanted but couldn't seem to make it happen during my growing-up years. One caveat or missing piece to this story is that I did not communicate and apologize for my behavior as an adolescent and young adult that was detrimental to our relationship, and I wish I had. Although this is a father-son story, it could be any combination of parent and young adult child. And it could be your story as a parent.

My mentor at the University of Wisconsin, Carl Whitaker, a well-known family psychiatrist, said on one occasion, "Fathers and sons are a sorry lot because we have such difficulty connecting emotionally."[7] But the lessons from this story for fathers and mothers and their young adult children are many.

Carl Whitaker

1. The experience of expressing and affirming the love between a parent and young adult is a freeing experience and no less important for both sons and daughters and their parents.

2. The gap can be closed by either generation initiating the process, but it's important to do this without any preconditions or preconceptions.

3. Because relationships are reciprocal, when one moves to close the emotional gap of the relationship there is an invitation for the other to do the same.

4. We never know how much time we have to make this emotional connection.

CHAPTER 8

Healthy Separation— My Research

In large part as a result of my personal journey to address the distance in relation-

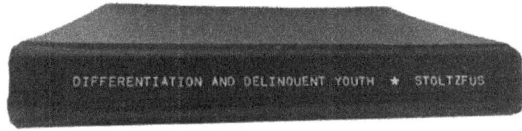

ship to my father, I undertook the task of defining and measuring healthy differentiation in adolescents. As noted earlier, I am using the terms *differentiation* or *individuation* as synonymous with emotional, psychological, and behavioral independence. The context was my PhD thesis at the University of Wisconsin that I completed in 1980. My interest at the time was in the adolescent or young adult experience of differentiation; however, as I progressed through my career, working more with parents and becoming a parent of three young adults, I have shifted my focus to understanding the concept of differentiation from the parent side. In other words, what can parents do to help adolescents and young adults attain healthy separation?

As with any research project, I began with a review of the literature. I found a strong emphasis on measures of independence. The literature often reflected the commonly held beliefs that differentiation consisted of behavioral characteristics such as financial independence, living independently from parents, maintaining a job, getting married, and eventually having a family. Historically in American society, completing high school or the equivalent was the start of adulthood.

There was less in the literature about emotional independence, implying if you have the former behavioral independence you were differentiated. At twenty-five years old, I had achieved behavioral independence but was clearly not differentiated emotionally from my father. My own experience and work with adolescents and college students who were struggling with feelings of anger, resentment, hurt, and sometimes fear, would argue for a broader definition that would consider the emotional connection or disconnection to the parents.

In 1976 I reached out to another psychiatrist, Murray Bowen, who had popularized the concept of "differentiation" in the family therapy literature of the seventies. I asked for his help in defining and measuring differentiation since he often referred to a scale of differentiation. He wrote back to me and discouraged my efforts by saying, "The concept of differentiation of self is too complex for a simple instrument to measure . . ."[8] Not to be thwarted in my quest, I continued to search literature for a measure of differentiation as a high degree of connectedness and a high degree of separateness or autonomy.

I found myself drawn to the work of Dr. Lorna Benjamin in the department of psychiatry at the University of Wisconsin. She was developing an assessment tool entitled the Structural Analysis of Social Behavior (SASB) that measured the combination of affiliation (connectedness) and autonomy in parent-child relationships. This

Lorna Benjamin

instrument and her work mainly focused on measuring parent-child dynamics in complex clinical cases, such as those with personality disorders. However, I was able to utilize the instrument to demonstrate its value to distinguish between delinquent and nondelinquent relationships with parents.[9]

My task was to demonstrate that a group of nondelinquent adolescents would demonstrate a higher degree of differentiation (high affiliation and high autonomy) than a delinquent, drug-abusing group of adolescents. Using Dr. Benjamin's instrument I enlisted the participation of two different groups of adolescents. One group came from a church community and the other was participating in a chemical dependency day treatment program due to drug abuse and delinquent behavior. When reviewing the scores of the two groups on the SASB measure of autonomy alone, the delinquent adolescents scored significantly higher. This made some sense since these adolescents were typically acting out and had few rules and expectations at home. But when combining both autonomy and affiliation, the normal adolescents were significantly higher than the delinquents. So normal, nondelinquent adolescent behavior correlated with higher scores on the combination of expressed affiliation (connection) and autonomy with parents.

In addition, and to the point of how parents were perceived by these two groups, the nondelinquent group saw their parents as significantly higher on behaviors such as encouraging a separate identity, listening, confirming as okay, friendly, inviting, soothing, calming, and affirming competence. Parents of healthy or normal adolescents and young adults at the beginning of the launching stage, demonstrate the combination of connection (love) and emancipation. They were seen as letting go in love.

The following chart describes the healthy behavior of parents and young adults who have achieved this state of connected independence. The behaviors are based upon the SASB with some expansion.

Parent behaviors	Young adult behaviors
Expressing unconditional love	Showing love and caring for parents
Encouraging separate identity	Establishing a separate identity
Expressing a belief in the young adult's competence	Demonstrating competence
Listening and carefully considering the young adult's views	Sharing, assertive and self disclosing without defensiveness or passivity
Demonstrating empathy	Showing concern and empathy for parents
Nurturing, soothing, and comforting expressions	Responding positively to parents calming and comforting expressions
Showing trust and ability to count on young adult	Exhibiting trust and ability to count on parent
Welcoming and friendly	Welcoming and friendly

Carl Whitaker described that a healthy, intimate relationship or marriage requires a high degree of "I-ness" and a high degree of "we-ness."[10] The same can be said of the parent-young adult relationship. Although these may seem contradictory, the challenge is to manage the dynamic. Sometimes closeness is emphasized, and sometimes distance or allowance for independence is emphasized. When not managed well it may feel like the parent and young adult are dancing to different music. One moves closer and the other moves further away. An emphasis on either to the exclusion of the other could jeopardize the relationship. This is why just creating distance or separation with the young adult is not enough to lead to a healthy separation. This book focuses on the "we-ness" side of the parent-young adult relationship. Later books in the series will focus more on supporting the "I-ness" side of healthy relationships. We seek support for both in relationships.

Sue Johnson wrote a book describing the emotionally focused marital relationship that is based in large part on recognizing that intimate adult relationships are basically attempts at meeting attachment needs.[11] This is no less true for parents and young adults who continue to value and seek to meet attachment needs. The list of questions below are derived from Johnson's work and adapted to parent-young adult relationships.

Sue Johnson

How do you think your young adult would answer these questions?

- Can they reach you? Are you accessible or too busy and difficult to contact?

- Do you tune in, attend, and really listen when they are disclosing their thoughts and feelings?

- Do you let them know they matter to you?

- Can they rely on you to respond to them emotionally? Will you shut them out or ignore or minimize their feelings?

- Can they count on you staying close to them emotionally, no matter what?

28

CHAPTER 9

Ask Your Young Adult— Your Story

One of the strategies that I introduce as part of my Parents Letting Go workshop is that of conducting an interview with the young adult. Rather than guess what your young adult is thinking or feeling or make assumptions based upon their actions, why not ask them? The set of questions you could use in such an interview are based on Sue Johnson's work but expanded to incorporate the "I-ness" feature of healthy relationships. Depending on the tone or comfort of the relationship you have with your young adult, their reception to the idea of a structured interview may be varied.

If you are in a situation where your young adult would be receptive, indicate to them that you are trying to learn how you can be a better parent and specifically how you could better demonstrate your love for them. Then ask them if they would be willing to answer a set of ten questions. You could propose going out for a meal and spending an hour or so eating while you interview them.

Indicate the goals:

- Understand your young adult better.

- Learn how you can be a better parent.

- Build a stronger relationship with them.

Assure them that you will:

- Not share their responses with anyone else unless you get their permission.

- Do your best to practice good listening by reflecting back what you hear to check for accurate understanding and promise not to interrupt or jump in with your reaction or opinion. You are meeting with them to learn.

- Not be judgmental or use the information against them now or in the future.

- Allow them to pass on any questions they feel uncomfortable answering.

It's very important to honor these conditions so the dialogue can contribute to improved communication between you and the young adult. Note also that each rating includes a follow-up question. This second question will help you learn how the rating could be improved. Ask them in each case what specific actions you could take to do better on that item. It's very important to ask the question as it is stated because it will cause your young adult to search in their thinking for ideas of what you can do differently. If you ask a simple yes or no question, such as "Do you have any suggestions of how I could do better on this quality?" you will elicit a yes or no response and most likely a "no" response. Asking open-ended questions will get your young adult to think more deeply, come up with meaningful suggestions, and lead to more valued dialogue over time.

Unconditional Love Expressions Quizzes

The two quizzes that follow are on the practice of unconditional love. The first version is to be answered by you as a parent as you believe your young adult would answer the questions. This will give you an idea of how well you think you do in expressing unconditional love in the eyes of your young adult. The second version is to be answered by your young adult and contains follow up questions to each rating.

Once you have each competed the quiz, meet to discuss any gaps or differences in your ratings. Find those with the largest gaps and discuss the suggestions they made in the follow-up question. If they didn't make any suggestions, ask them for one or two ideas of how you can close the gap between your answers and theirs. Make a commitment before you leave the discussion to work on one or more of the suggestions your young adult has made.

Taking the quiz yourself is likely not threatening but may be revealing in ways that are uncomfortable. However, moving beyond your own impressions of their answers to inviting their participation can be more uncomfortable and threatening to both you and your young adult. There are some helpful ideas in the earlier book available on this website. The book is entitled *Can You Speak Millennial "ese"* and provides guidance in how to approach your young adult, how to use nonjudgmental listening, and how to ask for feedforward (suggestions to facilitate the important dialogue you want to have with your young adult).

Parent Self Quiz on Unconditional Love

Please answer the following questions regarding the extent to which you believe these characteristics are true in your relationship with your young adult. Use a rating scale of 1-10:

| 0 | 1 | 2 | 3 | 4 | 5 | 6 | 7 | 8 | 9 | 10 |

completely not true   somewhat true and false   completely true

1. You believe your young adult can get your attention when they want to. _____

2. You believe you try to show that you want to listen and understand them. _____

3. You tell or show them that you think they are important to you. _____

4. You show acceptance of their feelings and emotions without ignoring them or being judgmental. _____

5. You allow them to be different from you in your beliefs, values, feelings, and actions. _____

6. You show unconditional love for them because they are your children regardless of their achievements or shortcomings. _____

7. You allow them to develop and have their own identity. _____

8. You allow and support their freedom and independence while staying connected to them. _____

9. You allow them to make mistakes and fail while continuing to love and accept them. _____

10. You show a willingness to listen, consider, change your mind, and otherwise be influenced by them while maintaining your values and beliefs. _____

Young Adult Quiz on Unconditional Love

Please answer the following questions regarding your view of your parent's relationship with you and approach to you. Use a rating scale of 1-10:

0	1	2	3	4	5	6	7	8	9	10

completely not true   somewhat true and false   completely true

After each rating offer suggestions of ways your parent can better demonstrate the quality or behavior you just rated.

1. I believe I am able to get your attention when I want to. _____

   - What one or two things could your parent say or do that would increase this score?

2. I believe you try to show that you want to listen and understand me. _____

   - What one or two things could your parent say or do to improve on this?

3. You tell or show me that you think I am important to you. _____

   - What one or two ways could your parent show you that you are important to them?

4. You show acceptance of my feelings and emotions without ignoring them or being judgmental. _____

   - What one or two ways could your parent do better at accepting your feelings?

5. You allow me to be different from you in my beliefs, values, feelings, and actions._____

   - What one or two ways could your parent improve in this area?

6. You show unconditional love for me because I am your child regardless of my achievements or shortcomings. _____

   - What one or two ways could your parent do better at showing unconditional love for you?

7. You allow me to develop my own identity. _____

   - What one or two ways could your parent do better at this?

8. You allow and support my freedom and independence while still connecting to me. _____

   - What one or two ways could your parent allow you more freedom and independence?

9. You allow me to make mistakes and fail while continuing to love and accept me. _____

   - What one or two ways could your parent do better on this?

10. You show a willingness to listen, consider, change your mind, and otherwise be influenced by me while maintaining your values and beliefs. _____

   - What ways could your parent do better on this?

Note: If both parents are available to the young adult, I recommend having the one-to-one conversation to review your responses and theirs separately. Each parent and young adult need to find the path forward toward greater love and freedom. Each parent and the dynamics between that parent and young adult are different and may need to be addressed in different ways.

Resistance to the Interview

These interview questions have the potential of surfacing perceptions and emotions that may be uncomfortable for both the parent and the young adult. This may lead to procrastination, ambivalence, or outright refusal to meet and answer these questions on the part of the young adult. The goal ultimately is to communicate your unconditional love for your young adult regardless of whether they answer a set of interview questions or not. It's important to keep this goal in mind and not try to force an exchange on this subject if they are unwilling. Here are some suggestions.

1. Offer reassurance that your intent is not to challenge, judge, or criticize any response they give. Suggest if you do, you will give them one or five bucks each time you slip. Practice your nonjudgmental listening before you start—it could cost you if you don't. See book one *Can You Speak Millennial "ese"?* for help with nonjudgmental listening. Review the purpose and conditions for the interview above.

2. Offer to treat them to breakfast, lunch, or dinner. Meet somewhere outside of your house. Getting something to eat or just coffee together creates more of an adult-to-adult venue. Sitting in your house can feel more parent-child like. This is great practice for the type of adult-to-adult relationship you want to have with them eventually. Maybe some time they will even buy!

3. Offer lots of options when requesting an opportunity to interview them. They can answer some questions, all the questions, do it now or a later date, in person or other—phone, email, and so forth. Ask them for ways you can understand them better if they refuse to do the interview. Allow them to say no, and then step back and try to communicate via email or text your desire to learn and understand them better. Given a written communication, they may pause to think before just saying "no."

4. Note: Don't be afraid or hesitant to use your young adult's preferred or common communication vehicles to connect with them.

> *"I have had more in depth communication with my son through email once he was away at college than I ever got when he was living at home."*
> —Parent of a college student

5. A study conducted at the University of Kansas (Metz Howard)[12] points to the value of multiple channels of communication. The study looked at the multiple forms of communications college students use—landlines, cell phones, texting, instant messaging, Snapchat, email, video calls, social networking sites (i.e. Facebook), and online gaming networks. College students average around three different preferred channels of communication. The study found that adding a channel of communication can improve the relationship with your young adult significantly.

If your young adult continues to refuse to respond to the questions, just back off. Work on changing your behavior and let go of getting them to move forward on your timetable.

CHAPTER 10

Parents Need to Step Up!

Parents have a responsibility to step up and close the gap that might exist between them and their young adults by expressing unconditional love. You may be facing an angry, rejecting, blaming, withdrawing, or otherwise challenging young adult. This does not excuse you from acting in love. You may naturally feel inclined to back away, defend, or point out the shortcomings of your young adult. This is a natural feeling and action since, as noted above, relationships are inherently reciprocal. You treat me badly; I will treat you badly. This describes the state of negative enmeshment. You are fused or enmeshed through negative emotions. You don't have to stay there.

How will this change unless you make efforts to shift the relationship and interactions toward a more positive end? If you stay defensive, angry, and rejecting of your young adult, why would you think their behavior would change in any way? This is the popular definition of insanity—continuing to do the same thing and expecting different results. Is it easy to shift toward a more loving approach? No! It's difficult. But parents need to step up, model, and work toward shifting the tone and quality of the relationship and expressing love, particularly unconditional love as a major step in that direction.

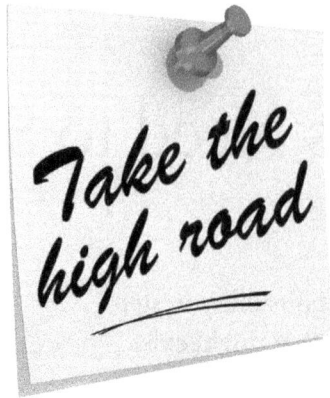

Take the high road

Parents: Take the high road, it's less crowded. Don't wait for the young adult to do this. For some parents and families, the verbal expression of love for family members is quite common. It is repeated so much it almost loses its meaning. "Please pass the butter, I love you." Unlike my family where such expressions were not that common, verbalizing this love may not have the same effect as it did in my experience. Other expressions of this love may be necessary to reinforce the message. It's not enough to just verbalize it. Actions that support the message are critical or the words become hollow. It's important as parents that you have and exhibit the right mindset and heartfelt attributes that will ensure that your specific actions are well received.

CHAPTER 11

Critical Parental Attributes

Demonstrating unconditional love, as well as the other practices that help parents with the launching process, requires certain attributes. Use the following attributes to deliver the message; it will help the message be received as sincere and heartfelt. Spend a little time thinking about how you can employ these qualities into the message and actions that communicate unconditional love for your young adult. Also, it's important to note to apply these attributes to how you treat yourself to counteract the tendency toward self-blame and guilt.

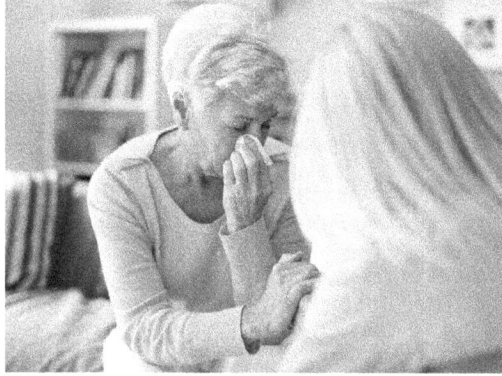

Vulnerability

In her writings and Ted Talk in 2010, Brene Brown describes vulnerability as "the language of intimacy."[13] Intimacy involves risk. We can't expect to connect to our young adults unless we soften our hearts and risk our own vulnerability. If we hold on to an attitude of needing to be strong, right, in control, unemotional, rational, and unapologetic, there is little likelihood that any efforts, no matter how sophisticated, will ensure we make the connection we desire with our young adults. We can't ask them deep personal questions regarding their perceptions and feelings toward us if we are not willing to share these same feelings and perceptions with them through an open, nonblaming heart.

39

We need to begin our efforts to reach out to our young adults with an admission that we have made mistakes in raising them and are sincerely sorry for this. We can indicate we can't change the past but we can try to do better in the future. Then when we follow with a desire to get to know them better, the invitation clearly comes from the heart and not from some disguised place of manipulation.

Compassion

Compassion is defined as an empathetic awareness of another's distress with a desire to alleviate it. If you have had an easy transition through the young adult years, it may be difficult to identify with your young adult's struggles. It is important to understand and accept that they are different, and this time in life is possibly more challenging than it was for us. It's important to recognize that their behavior, whether deviating from our expectations or in some way antagonistic to our expectations of them, is their effort to grow in the areas of identity, independence, and intimacy.

We have to see past the external behavior and attitudes to listen to their pain and insecurities without judging or attempting to control. Compassion allows the other to face the consequences of their actions but expresses a desire to help them bear the emotional impact. Spend some time getting in touch with your own adolescent/young adult experience and some of the challenges you faced to be able to empathize with them. Compassion is connecting at the heart level.

Patience

Today the pace of moving through the young adult years is much slower, and the achievement of the typical milestones of young adulthood is prolonged. This is in contrast to the speed of change and the hyperkinetic culture we live in where we may feel paralyzed with the overwhelming choices and options we have in all areas of our lives. Life is much more complex these days.

Employment in a desired career has been difficult; most young adults graduating from college have more than forty thousand in debt. This is the first generation where the expectation is that they will not do as well financially as their parents. Sixty-five percent are currently employed. Half are employed part time. Twenty percent live under the poverty level.

Today's young adults are getting married later than our generation. Males are getting married for the first time at the average age of twenty-nine, and females are marrying for the first time at twenty-seven. I would argue they are much smarter than us boomers who married young and divorced at the rate of more than fifty percent. Today's rate of divorce is thirty-two percent and may in part be related to getting married later in life. By twenty-seven and twenty-nine, young adults have worked through some of necessary tasks of identity and independence that enable them to bring a more mature self to the marriage. Our experience was different and not necessarily better or worse. But it's a mistake and a lack of compassion (empathy) to approach our young adults based upon how we navigated the young adult journey. The journey to achieve certain adult milestones may take longer than it took for us. Try to think of today's young adults as different and not delayed in their development. For some parents, the mantra "this too shall pass" is what gives them the most hope.

Acceptance and Forgiveness

It's important to demonstrate our acceptance of our young adults' efforts to attain young adulthood, even though the route they take may not be something we would have taken. This is an important quality to cultivate in effective parenting of young adults—the ability to support the underlying drives for identity, independence, and intimacy while not necessarily supporting their decisions on how to accomplish these developmental tasks. And it's terribly important to allow them to make mistakes and not intervene to prevent this because you rob them of one of the most important sources of learning. Madeline Levine in *The Price of Privilege* makes a strong case for not overindulging our young adults or protecting them from consequences.[14]

Finally, it's important to forgive them for decisions and actions that have failed since we all have made mistakes. Do you just keep forgiving? Yes! But forgiving is not condoning behavior. Nor is it supporting destructive behavior. I've worked with some parents whose young adult has been through multiple, failed chemical dependency treatment programs often at great expenses to the parents. But we can't stop trying and stop forgiving their failures to finally overcome a devastating problem such as addiction. For more on forgiveness, see the next book in this series, *Apology: The Gift We Give Our Young Adults.*

Gratitude

Having a mindset of gratitude helps us to maintain balance when it seems like the young adult is failing or exhibiting irresponsible behaviors. If you have a very contentious relationship or have experienced many disappointments with your young adult, gratitude may be difficult. But the challenge is to find the value, the strengths, and the positive qualities with your young adult and call them out with gratitude. As young adults go through tough times, they need to know we are so grateful we have them, that they exist, and that they matter. Practicing gratitude enables us to have a more balanced view when things are not going well.

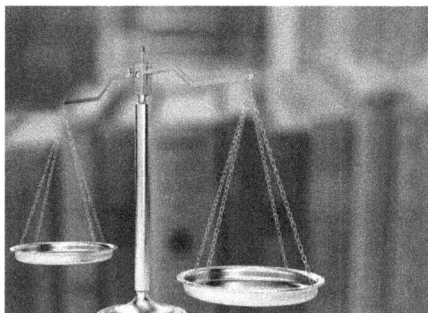

We can help them more by identifying and affirming their strengths than by pointing out their weaknesses and mistakes. The latter cause them to pull away in anger and shut us out. The former cause them to gain confidence and lean toward us for continued reinforcement and affirmation. You win the right to be heard when you recognize them as your special, unique, talented, and loved adult child. The next chapter describes specific actions you can take to connect to your feelings of love and express them in different ways.

> "He is a wise man who does not grieve for the things which he has not, but rejoices for those which he has." —Epictetus

42

CHAPTER 12

Overcoming Barriers to Unconditional Love

Many things can stand in the way of expressing unconditional love even though we believe it is the right thing to do. It's important for parents to adopt certain beliefs regarding unconditional love.

One barrier for some parents is they feel so hurt and rejected by their young adults that they find it hard to be loving. In this case it is important to remind ourselves to separate the behavior from the person. It's also important to recognize that these young people are trying their best, sometimes in strange or inappropriate ways, to establish their identity and independence and address their needs for intimacy outside the house.

Sometimes going back in your memory and seeing the little boy or girl you held as an infant can help you reconnect with those feelings of love and attachment. Although expressing unconditional love can change your heart, is not primarily for you but for them. It may require you to override your feelings to speak to the deeper desire you have to love them. Reaching out in love to them without expectations of a payoff or specific response is our responsibility as a parent. By expressing this love accompanied by appropriate acts of kindness you will find your heart softening.

> *"I never experienced unconditional love in my growing up; how can I show this to my adult children?"* —a client

Another barrier may be a parent's own experience in growing up. It's not unusual for my clients to speak of not hearing messages or seeing actions of unconditional love from their parents. My response is that they don't get a pass because they didn't get something from their parents or their parents were abusive. The client, whose statement is above, was able to experience unconditional love through an aunt and grandparent, so she does know something about this firsthand. Another client grew up with an alcoholic father who beat him regularly. He said he learned what he never wanted to be or do as a parent and has treated his kids, both young adults now, with unconditional love and affection. Sometimes we can learn what not to do from experiences with our parents as much as we can learn what to do.

Attitudes and feelings also can become barriers to a parent's expression of unconditional love and ultimately to letting go of one's young adult. If you are angry, blaming, rejecting, punishing, and demanding, it will be hard to move toward expressing the unconditional love that is necessary to affirm and emancipate your young adult. It's important to let go of these feelings that will ultimately bind you and your young adult in a negative enmeshed state. These feelings and the accompanying actions will trigger similar feelings and reactions from the young adult and will drive the relationship to an increasing negative downward spiral. This was what had come to characterize my relationship with my father in my early young adult years.

Even though you may have reasons to be angry at your young adult for inappropriate behavior or treatment of you, holding on to this and not expressing the underlying feeling of love that exists in spite of your young adult's actions will be damaging to both of you. The next book in this series, *I Did the Best I Could*, deals with ways to overcome these emotions and others, such as fear, anxiety, and guilt.

Parents who have been raised in stoic environments where expressions of affection and love were not practiced may find it hard to reach out to their young adult and express this unconditional love. These parents may feel like it's a sign of weakness to admit to having this enduring love for the child. It may feel too vulnerable. Or in some cases there is the fear the young adult may try to take advantage of this admission to extract certain concessions. Neither my father nor the burly father in the example at the beginning of this book had learned to verbally express this unconditional love. But in both cases, the love was there but never communicated. In the case of my father who grew up on a farm, there wasn't a practice of his father communicating love or affection for him or his siblings. Such a lack of verbal expression and affection clearly characterize certain cultures and heritages. These stoic homes remind me of the popular story of the wife who after twenty years of marriage asks her husband if he loves her and he replies: "I said it once when we were married and will let you know if that ever changes." Saying it once is not enough either for spouses or sons and daughters.

Most attendees at my workshop want to know how to help their young adult; however, this is often code for "how can I get them to change" in a direction that I believe is right or better. Then this becomes a barrier because parents want a quick answer and there are no quick and foolproof answers. We have to remind ourselves of certain assumptions or truths.

- We cannot control our young adults.

- We are not responsible for their decisions or actions.

- We are responsible for our decisions and actions.

- We need to change first to show the change we want in our relationship.

Will my actions make a difference?

Keep in mind that the only person we can change is oneself. My desire is for you to feel less guilt and fear, and sleep better at night knowing that you are taking the best actions you can as a parent. Will this lead to a change in the relationship with our young adult? The answer is yes, because your actions will be different and if one party changes the relationship changes. However, like changing one's dance step midstream without telling your partner, the results may not be pretty. Your young adult may become more resistant initially or be confused by the change in your approach.

Change is often awkward at the outset. In addition, because relationships are inherently reciprocal, there is some likelihood that they will change in a positive way as well. But if you express love with the assumption you will impact the actions of your young adult or they will reciprocate, you are not acting unconditionally. Your goal and expectations should be related to being the parent you want to be regardless of the response from your young adult. So the relationship has to change. Love breeds love and kindness breeds kindness.

> "One of the most difficult things to give away is kindness (love); it usually comes back to you. " —Anonymous

Sometimes, however, your young adult doesn't reciprocate or respond in kind. No matter how hard you try, your son or daughter may pull away and choose to not have a relationship with you.

Quite a few parents in my practice are suffering from this cutoff and are experiencing a lot of emotional pain. What factors are likely to make the difference in whether or not your young adult changes?

- Your ability to connect to them through a sincere expression of your unconditional love.

- Your ability to persist at demonstrating this as well as other practices described in other books in the series.

- Your young adult's receptivity and willingness to stay connected and make changes that reflect an individuated position—high affiliation and high autonomy.

CHAPTER 13

Expressing Unconditional Love—The Letter

Reconnect with the feelings of affection and unconditional love

1. Take some time to reconnect to feelings that you experienced when your adult child was an infant or young child. It might help to pull out old pictures and movies and observe your child and your interactions with them. Try to reconnect to those feelings and realize that the little boy or girl is still in there but in a grown-up form.

2. List the "being" qualities of your young adult. These are hard-wired qualities such as personality, temperament, intelligence, capabilities, and demonstrated strengths. Add to these the actions or the "doing" qualities of learned skills, accomplishments, and achievements that have made you proud of your young adult over the years. Reread these from time to time to balance off any current issues or behaviors that concern you. No child or young adult is all bad or all good. Neither are we as parents. Having balance is important.

3. Go down memory lane and review materials and awards you have saved from your young adult's school and extracurricular activities.

4. Make a gratitude list of ways you are grateful that this child has been in your life.

Express your unconditional love

Write a letter to your young adult with the first draft being for your benefit. This will help clarify what you want to express and connect your heart to the young adult. Suggested themes:

- What you have appreciated about your young adult over the years?

- What has made you proud of them over the years, particularly areas of personal strength, care for others, persistence, humor, friendliness, and so forth?

- How you have benefited from having them in your life?

- What you have learned from them that has helped you?

- Describe the ways you love your child.

- Describe your unconditional love for your child from your heart. You can use guidance from this book and others you have read, but be sure it is your voice, sincere and from the heart.

- Reassure and promise that your unconditional love will be there no matter what.

- Apologize if you believe you have made mistakes. If there are some mistakes that your young adult still holds onto, write specifically to these.

- Forgive your young adult for behavior that the young adult has identified as mistakes or failures. This is particularly important if you believe your adult child is enmeshed with you due to a sense of failure or guilt. Don't forgive if the behavior is something only you believe is needing forgiveness. This could seem condescending. See the next book in this series, *I Did the Best I Could,* for help with forgiveness.

- Express your hopes, desires, and aspirations for your young adult without being prescriptive. At a minimum you want to say that you want them to be happy and fulfilled in life.

Read the letter out loud to hear how it sounds. Share the letter with your spouse or close friend to ensure that it is free of blaming or accusing. Check to be sure you did not say, "I love you, *but*" or

"I'm sorry, *but*." The "but" in these statements negates the first part of the statement and will suggest that you really don't love unconditionally and really aren't sorry. Also don't use the politician's apology: "I'm sorry if you feel you were mistreated in growing up." This is a nonapology apology.

After you have edited and discussed the letter with your spouse, a friend, or a professional, then prepare to communicate this to your young adult. You can do this in writing, and if you do, I would suggest using the old fashioned way of writing a personal letter. Even though our millennial population is digital and media savvy, there is something about a handwritten letter that sends a more personal message. One parent cautioned me that today's generation may not be able to read cursive, particularly if your penmanship is like mine, pretty awful. This never occurred to me. What happened to penmanship? Well if you saw my writing you would probably ask the same question. So I typed my letter to my kids.

If you can muster the courage, the best approach is to take your young adult out to eat or for a walk and read the letter to them. In my experience as a therapist, when parents share such a letter, it is quite emotional for the parent and sometimes for the young adult, but always impactful. Here are a few excerpts from letters I collected from parents over the years.

"I want you to know that I love you—I always have and always will—no matter what has happened in the past or will happen in the future. You mean the world to me and that will never change. I will always be here for you."

One father called out certain qualities that his son, an Eagle Scout, has that will enable him to be successful in his life but also focused on his "being" traits: *"Your traits of empathy, persistence, and intelligence will help you be successful in your drive for independence."*

A mother wrote: *"I love you with all my heart—no matter what—unconditionally. I am so proud of you and all of your accomplishments. You have such a big heart. I will always be in your heart and just a thought way."* This mother communicated her presence with her daughter in an interesting way—not that the daughter will always be in the mother's heart but that the mother will always be in the daughter's heart, a thought away. A way of saying I will always be with you.

From a parent of a young adult with mental illness diagnosis: "*You will be living with this (the mental health problem) all your life even after your dad and I are no longer on this earth. We realize we are part of the problem with our control issues and trying to steer you forward and sometimes we see the light at the end of the tunnel but you only see an oncoming train. There will always be good and bad days (in life) but we will always love you unconditionally and with all our hearts.*"

When you have prepared to communicate your unconditional love for your young adult, you need to approach your child and indicate you want to share an important message with them. At that point, if you are with them and going to read the message to them, discuss your expectations of them.

- You will share some feelings and thoughts about them related to the past, present, and future.

- You ask them to listen (or read if sent) without interruption or comment until you have finished.

- Once you have finished reading or they have read this if sent, indicate that you have no expectation of any response from them. This would be totally up to them with one exception that they acknowledge they received your letter.

Then you have to mean what you said and not wait for or expect a response or bug them if they do not respond over time. I had one parent who sent a letter along these lines to his daughter and never got a response. Should he ask if the daughter got the letter? If he only asks the daughter to acknowledge the letter, that's fine. But it does suggest that the father was expecting something from his daughter. What he needs to do to drive the point of the letter is to have his actions support his words going forward. It's about his heart changing and the behavior following this—not about the response of the young adult. You have done what you can to communicate in writing your unconditional love for your young adult. By doing so, you are a better parent and can sleep better knowing no matter what the future brings they will be assured of your love.

Other Tangible Acts of Unconditional Love

Words are not enough. In fact, if your actions do not match your words you have introduced another damaging element into your relationship with your young adult—a hypocrisy or phoniness that will likely make things worse. So walk the talk. It's important that your actions arise out of love and what's best for the young adult and not out of fear, anger, a need to control, or what makes you feel better. When you are about to act, ask yourself: Is this action what is best to show both love and support for my young adult's independence?

How are you doing in the practice of communicating unconditional love and where could you "step up" your actions? Rate the extent to which the statements below describe you. And then indicate which ones you would be willing to implement in the next week. Don't try to overachieve. Choose one or two, and once these are mastered pick another one or two. It's not a race. It's a journey. Being intentional and consistent in what you do is more important than the quantity of actions. Use this rating scale:

0 = not at all descriptive
1 = somewhat descriptive
2 = fairly descriptive
3 = quite descriptive

My actions	My rating	What one or two actions will you consider to increase the rating?
Communicate verbally and/or in writing your unconditional love without any exceptions or "buts" or expectations of response.		
Practice asking yourself in each communication and action: Is this in the best interest of the young adult or is it more about what I want?		
Show affection unconditionally but not in a clinging or smothering way.		
Accept your young adult's feelings and not try to suggest that their feelings are untrue. Feelings are not to be challenged.		
Acknowledge and accept differences.		
Demonstrate empathy—listening to both emotions and content and reflect this back.		
Be emotionally present—tune in verbally and nonverbally without being distracted.		
Remain calm in the midst of conflict or attack and try to focus on understanding their position.		
Ask questions and show a genuine interest and openness to learn and understand them.		
Demonstrate openness, honesty, and vulnerability about your experience.		
Resist withholding love and affection based upon their behavior or mistakes they make.		
Communicate how your young adult matters and is important and valued by you.		
Show interest in what's important to them and seek to connect with them as adults—go out to eat, do activities, make symbolic gestures.		
Find an accountability partner, spouse or another parent, who will walk with you in this process.		

Which actions are you willing to work on in the next two weeks? Your best chance of coming through on any commitment is if you are accountable. And the one most able to indicate if you are following through on your commitments is your young adult. So indicate that you are going to be working on a couple of areas that relate to showing unconditional love. Check if they support the areas or actions that you will take or whether they might recommend one or two different ones. Indicate you will ask them weekly or every two weeks if they have observed your new actions. Also, when you check in with them, ask them if you could do something more or better to demonstrate love relative to one or more of these acts.

By using this approach, which is described in detail in *Can You Speak Millennial "ese,"* the first book in this series, you engage the young adult in your change process. This not only enables you to have more success in changing, but helps your young adult change in perception of you. Ultimately both changes support a closer relationship. Note: don't try to overachieve or take on too many changes at one time. The specific communication of love is important so if you have a question on this, make this your first assignment. Then add maybe two behaviors you will work on after the delivery of your unconditional love letter. Keep it simple and get into a rhythm of working on an action and checking with your young adult. Who knows, maybe at some point your young adult may ask if there are things they can do differently to help build a better relationship. But don't hold your breath.

CHAPTER 15

Your Assignment

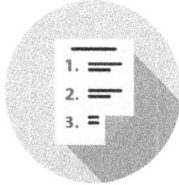

My goal	My action	My time period	Feedback from young adult*

*Reminder to ask whether your young adult observed your actions (feedback) and what further suggestions they have for how you could do better (feedforward).

CHAPTER 16

Keepers

My friend Terry Paulson, who is a leadership consultant, motivational speaker, and humorist, likes to have people identify "Keepers." These are key points, recommendations, and ideas that people take with them and apply after hearing a lecture or reading something. I will give you some ideas for keepers, but you may have something different that you want to take with you from this book. Please jot these down and apply them as soon as you can. If you don't, they will fade away like other things you have heard or read and intended to apply. Make a commitment to take at least one constructive action from this book and implement it within twenty-four hours.

1. To experience and know that one is loved unconditionally by a parent is essential for a young adult to leave the family in a healthy way. Love them to let them go.

2. Parents need to take the initiative and ensure that they communicate unconditional love through words and actions. Actions speak louder than words. Love in the context of this practice is a verb not a noun. Do it, don't just say it.

3. Recognize and try to understand late adolescent and young adult behavior in terms of a need to address developmental tasks of iden-

tity, independence, and intimacy. Don't take their effort to distance themselves from you to establish their identity as rejection.

4. Don't use or assume that your young adult will follow the same path that you took during your young adulthood, and if they don't something is wrong. Differences indicate their uniqueness and are not inherently good or bad. Embrace them.

5. Express gratitude for your young adult and call out positive character traits, strengths, personal qualities, and unique characteristics (their being) and not just achievements (their doing).

6. You can reach your young adult best through vulnerability—heart connections that acknowledge your mistakes; apologize and disclose your deepest desires for their happiness.

7. Approach your young adult out of what will be most loving and helpful to them in their development—identity, independence, and intimacy. Avoid acting out of your fear, hurt, anger, resentment, anxiety, guilt, or what will make you feel better.

8. Connect through compassion for their mistakes and failures, and stand with them in support of their learning.

9. Practice and model forgiveness and self-love for this is a gift they need to take with them in their journey of leaving home. Practicing unconditional love of self is a gift you can give yourself in letting go.

10. Practice acceptance that there are things you can't change or control and have patience because this process of separation is taking longer these days. Approach this stage of life with optimism and hope and a belief that there are better days ahead.

When our children were young, they stepped on our toes; we forgave them, said we loved them, and it would be okay. As young adults they make mistakes and step on our hearts; our words of forgiveness, love, and hope are just as important.

NOTES

1. Brene Brown, *The Gifts of Imperfection* (Center City, MN: Hazelden, 2010), 26.

2. Description given in personal conversation with Frank Farelly in 1978 while in Madison, Wisconsin. Frank Farelly is the author of *Provocative Therapy.*

3. Alfie Kohn, *Unconditional Parenting: Moving from Rewards and Punishments to Love and Reason* (New York: Simon and Schuster, 2005).

4. Daniel J. Seigel, *Mindsight* (New York: Random House, Inc., 2010).

5. Diane Kliebold, *A Mother's Reckoning* (New York: Crown Publishers, 2016).

6. Harold S. Kushner described forgiveness as the "favor you give yourself" in a Minnesota Public Radio broadcast in 2016.

7. Carl Whitaker, personal conversation while studying with Dr. Whitaker in 1975, Madison, Wisconsin.

8. Murray Bowen, personal correspondence, April 14, 1976.

9. Lorna Benjamin, *Interpersonal Diagnosis and Treatment of Personality Disorders*, 2nd ed. (New York: Guilford Press, 1996).

10. Carl Whitaker, personal conversation while studying with Dr. Whitaker in 1975, Madison, Wisconsin.

11. Sue Johnson, *Hold Me Tight: Seven Conversations for a Lifetime of Love* (New York: Little, Brown and Company, 2008).

12. Christine Metz Howard, "Relationships Benefit When Parents, Adult Children Connect through Multiple Channels." https://news.ku.edu/relationships-benefit-when-parents-connect-adult-children-through-multiple-communication-channels-0

13. Brene Brown, Ted Talk, https://www.ted.com/talks/brene_brown_on_vulnerability

14. Madeline Levine, *The Price of Privilege* (New York: Harper, 2008).